BRUMBACK LIBRARY

3 3045 00163 9372

 W9-CHA-685

$11.95

j599   Rappoport, Bernice
RAP   Baby animals

CHILDREN'S DEPARTMENT
THE BRUMBACK LIBRARY
OF VAN WERT COUNTY
VAN WERT, OHIO

Baby Animals

Written by Bernice Rappoport

Illustrated by Jean Cassels

TREASURE TREE™

World Book, Inc.
a Scott Fetzer company
Chicago   London   Sydney   Toronto

j599
RAP

Copyright © 1992
World Book, Inc.
525 West Monroe Street
Chicago, Illinois 60661

All rights reserved.
This volume may not be reproduced
in whole or in part in any form without
prior written permission from the publisher.

Printed in the United States of America
ISBN 0-7166-1621-1
Library of Congress Catalog Card No. 91-65748

8 9 10 11 12 13 14 15 99 98 97 96

Cover design by Rosa Cabrera
Book design by Lucy Smith

All babies have one thing in common. They have a lot of growing up to do! Just like you, animal babies learn from the grown-ups around them. The babies copy the grown-ups so they can do what they do. By watching their parents, baby animals learn what to eat, how to find food, and how to stay safe. Animal babies can be curious and playful little creatures. From the tiny mouse to the enormous elephant, all baby animals learn how to live like others of their kind.

When these baby mice were born, they had no fur and their eyes were closed. In two weeks' time, they grew from helpless creatures to furry, bright-eyed little mice. The babies feel safe and cozy in the nest made of leaves and grass. One baby mouse boldly wanders and explores.

Mice can hear and smell very well, but they cannot see very well. Whiskers help them feel what they cannot see. Whiskers can let the little explorer know that the hole is too small for it to enter. Is this a good time for it to return to the nest?

An egg is too small to hold a duckling that's ready to hatch. The shell can crack when the duckling moves inside it. Also, the duckling taps the shell with an egg tooth to make more cracks.

The new mallard ducklings rest and dry off. They look soft and fluffy when their down dries. In about two days, these two will be running, swimming, and finding their own food.

When mallard ducks are fully grown, the males' feathers will turn bright green during the mating season. The females' feathers, however, will always be brown.

At birth, baby beavers look like their parents. Within a few hours they can swim. Beavers move more easily in the water than they do on land. They have webbed back feet and a flat tail to propel and steer them through the water. Unlike you, beavers don't have to worry about getting water in their noses or ears. They can close those openings with a special muscle. They even have a pair of clear eyelids so that they can see underwater.

These busy beavers are making a dam.
No one taught the baby beavers how to
gnaw trees, gather the twigs, and build. That
comes as naturally to a beaver as swimming.
There is one thing beavers will never learn—
how to tell which way a tree is going to fall!

These cottontail rabbits feel playful. Even so, they are always on the lookout. If danger is near, they might hop away in a zigzag. That makes them hard to catch. Or they may stay as still as a statue in the grass so that they are hard to see.

These babies are cleaning themselves and getting their vitamins at the same time! As they lick themselves clean, the sun heats an oil in their fur. The oil becomes a vitamin. Rabbits wash carefully. They even clean between their toes. How do you keep your hair neat? Can you guess what rabbits brush their fur with? They use their paws.

When baby opossums are born, they
are no bigger than honey bees! They
cannot hear or see, and they have no fur.
Yet, they are able to find their way to their
mother's pouch.

Do you think it would be fun to be
carried around like these young opossums?
Sometimes it's not easy to climb aboard
mother's back.

Opossums live on the ground or in
trees, and they eat most anything. To be
safe from other animals, opossums have
a special trick. They play dead!

When these baby raccoons were born,
you couldn't see the masks on their faces or the
rings on their tails. Now, they can't be missed!

Raccoons can do amazing things with their paws.
They have such long fingers that they can pick things
up, catch fish, dig, and climb trees.

Sometimes baby raccoons get stuck in trees. When
that happens, their mothers have to fetch them. You
see, it's easier for them to climb up than down.

What's the first thing you see when you look at a porcupine? Is it the quills? When porcupines are born, their quills are soft.

Porcupines use their quills to protect themselves. Any animal that gets too close to a porcupine might get a mouthful of quills. A frightened porcupine will turn around and slap the other animal with its tail. The quills are sharp and barbed, so when they brush across the animal's face, the quills stick. When porcupines are not frightened, they are very gentle animals.

Kangaroos are tiny when they are born. Like opossum babies, they find their way into their mothers' pouch. They aren't ready to leave the pouch for months.

When kangaroo babies, or joeys, leave the pouch for the first time, it is only for a moment. Each time after that, they stay out longer. By eight months old, joeys are ready to live outside the pouch.

Joeys that live outside the pouch can play together because kangaroos live together in groups called mobs.

Each year, emperor penguins travel across Antarctica. They return to their breeding grounds to lay and hatch eggs.

Fathers warm the eggs night and day for eight weeks, while the mothers get food. The mothers return when the chicks are ready to hatch. Both parents take care of their chicks.

When the chicks get a little older, they can be left alone while their parents find food.

Like all polar bears, these cubs were born in winter. They had no fur and could not see. They stayed close to their mother in their den under the snow. When spring came, their mother led them outside for the first time. The cubs' thick, white fur keeps them warm and hidden. Like you, cubs like to romp and play. Soon the playful cubs will be learning how to hunt seals.

As evening falls, the mother tiger and her cubs set off to find dinner. The mother tiger will hide her cubs in the tall grasses, while she hunts alone. When the cubs get older, they will watch and follow her.

Did you know that playing together helps cubs become hunters? That's because when tiger cubs play, they run and jump and stalk one another. Those are the kinds of things they will do when they are hunters.

Baby camels can stand up and walk shortly after birth, but they are a bit wobbly. A wide pad on the bottom of each foot helps hold camels on top of the sand.

Do camels fall and scrape the hair from their knees? No. They are born with bare spots on their legs. Then the skin grows tougher. This makes kneeling down and standing up in the sand easier.

Camels don't get sand in their eyes, even on the windiest days. They have long eyelashes that lock together when camels close their eyes. They also have a third eyelid that wipes dust off their eyes.

Elephants' trunks are amazing. They can do the work of both your nose and arms. Elephants use their trunks to smell and touch, and to get food and water. They can even blast their trunks like a trumpet. Baby elephants' trunks are too short to be of much use. If their trunks were longer, they wouldn't be able to drink their mothers' milk.

Mothers use their trunks to take care of both themselves and their babies. Mothers can shower their children or guide them to the water with their trunks. How could a mother elephant hug her child?

Whose Baby Are You?
Match each mother to its baby.

More About Baby Animals

The baby birds and mammals in this book are all warm-blooded vertebrates. These animals' body temperature remains stable throughout the day, whatever the temperature, and they all have backbones. They live in different parts of the world. Each in its own way is well suited to its environment.

Birds: Feathers, and not the ability to fly, distinguish a bird from other types of animals. Penguins are flightless birds. They use their wings to propel them through the water.

Mammals: The animals in this group share the following characteristics:

1) Mothers supply milk for their babies.
2) The babies are given more care and protection than most other animals.
3) They have hair.
4) They have larger and more well-developed brains than other animals.

Marsupials: This subgroup of mammals is distinguished from other mammals because their babies are born less fully developed. The newborns grow in their mothers' pouches.

Rodents: These mammals have front teeth that are designed for gnawing hard objects. They have one pair of upper incisors. These teeth wear away more rapidly in the back than the front, so they become chisellike. The incisors continue to grow throughout most of a rodent's life.

Lagomorphs: This group includes rabbits. Like rodents, lagomorphs are gnawers with chisellike incisors. Lagomorphs, however, have two pairs of upper incisors. The word comes from the Greek, *lagomorpha*, which means "hare-shaped."

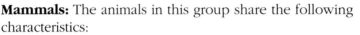

To Parents

Children delight in hearing and reading about animal babies. *Baby Animals* will provide your child with interesting information about a number of these as well as a bridge into learning some important concepts. Here are a few easy and natural ways your child can express feelings and understandings about the baby animals in the book. You know your child and can best judge which ideas he or she will enjoy most.

Animals have unique ways of moving, walking, and talking. Children enjoy mimicking animals. Pretend to be a duckling by stooping down, holding onto your ankles, and flapping arms as you say "peep, peep." Ask your child to guess what animal you are. Encourage your child to choose another baby animal to mimic.

Guessing games can be used with the information in the book to present animal facts. Play the game "Who Am I?" Start by giving a clue about a baby animal, such as, "I have a very long nose—who am I?" Add more clues until your child names the animal. Then ask your child to find the animal's picture in the book. Reverse the action and let your child give clues.

Animals have many characteristics that are alike and that can be used to group or classify animals. With your child, make a chart by writing *Animals* on the top right

and these characteristics on the left: *Can fly, Can swim, Can walk, Can run.* Then go through the book writing each name in each row that tells what the animal can do.

A delightful way to add new words to your child's vocabulary is by using the pictures in the book. Choose a baby animal and invite your child to describe it. Then help your child use other colorful words to describe the animal. For example, a soft rabbit; a fluffy rabbit; a fuzzy rabbit; a velvety rabbit. Help your child write down the words as you think of them.

Invite your child to become an author. Think of a baby animal that was not included in the book. Help your child write several things about the animal, patterning the article after the ones in the book. Use a reference book if necessary. Draw pictures or use magazine pictures to illustrate. Then bind the pages into a book to share with others.